50 Peruvian Ceviche and Cocktail Recipes for Home

By: Kelly Johnson

Table of Contents

- Classic Peruvian Ceviche
- Mixed Seafood Ceviche
- Fisherman's Ceviche
- Scallop and Shrimp Ceviche
- Octopus Ceviche
- Spicy Tuna Ceviche
- Mango and Avocado Ceviche
- Coconut Milk Ceviche
- Ceviche Tostadas
- Ceviche Tacos
- Ceviche Stuffed Avocado
- Ceviche Lettuce Wraps
- Ceviche Stuffed Mini Peppers
- Ceviche Rice Bowls
- Ceviche Salad
- Passion Fruit Ceviche
- Quinoa Ceviche Salad
- Peruvian Ceviche Soup
- Peruvian Ceviche Pizza
- Peruvian Ceviche Spring Rolls
- Peruvian Ceviche Empanadas
- Peruvian Ceviche Sushi Rolls
- Peruvian Ceviche Nachos
- Peruvian Ceviche Crostinis
- Peruvian Ceviche Bruschetta
- Peruvian Ceviche Stuffed Potato Skins
- Peruvian Ceviche Lettuce Cups
- Peruvian Ceviche Tostones
- Peruvian Ceviche Skewers
- Peruvian Ceviche Sandwiches
- Peruvian Ceviche Wraps
- Peruvian Ceviche Canapés
- Peruvian Ceviche Dip
- Peruvian Ceviche Cucumber Bites
- Peruvian Ceviche Sopes

- Peruvian Ceviche Wontons
- Peruvian Ceviche Bruschetta
- Peruvian Ceviche Pinchos
- Peruvian Ceviche Pita Pockets
- Peruvian Ceviche Sliders
- Peruvian Ceviche Flatbreads
- Peruvian Ceviche Popsicles
- Peruvian Ceviche Stuffed Mushrooms
- Peruvian Ceviche Potato Salad
- Peruvian Ceviche Deviled Eggs
- Peruvian Ceviche Gazpacho
- Peruvian Ceviche Sushi Bowls
- Peruvian Ceviche Sopes
- Peruvian Ceviche Bruschetta
- Peruvian Ceviche Stuffed Jalapeños

Classic Peruvian Ceviche

Ingredients:

- 1 lb fresh white fish fillets (such as sea bass, sole, or tilapia), diced into bite-sized pieces
- 1 cup freshly squeezed lime juice
- 1 red onion, thinly sliced
- 1-2 hot peppers (aji amarillo or jalapeño), seeded and finely chopped
- 1-2 cloves garlic, minced
- 1/4 cup chopped cilantro
- 1-2 tomatoes, seeded and diced
- Salt, to taste
- Pepper, to taste
- Corn kernels (optional)
- Sweet potato, boiled and sliced (optional)
- Lettuce leaves (for serving)

Instructions:

In a large glass or ceramic bowl, combine the diced fish with the lime juice. Make sure the fish is completely submerged in the lime juice. Cover the bowl with plastic wrap and refrigerate for about 20-30 minutes. The fish should become opaque and "cooked" in the lime juice.

While the fish is marinating, prepare the other ingredients. Thinly slice the red onion, finely chop the hot peppers, mince the garlic, chop the cilantro, and dice the tomatoes.

After the fish has marinated, drain off most of the lime juice, leaving just a little to keep the ceviche moist. Add the sliced red onion, chopped hot peppers, minced garlic, chopped cilantro, and diced tomatoes to the bowl with the fish.

Season the ceviche with salt and pepper, to taste. Gently toss all the ingredients together until well combined.

If desired, add corn kernels and sliced boiled sweet potato to the ceviche for extra flavor and texture.

To serve, line a serving platter or individual plates with lettuce leaves. Spoon the ceviche onto the lettuce leaves and garnish with additional cilantro leaves, if desired.

Enjoy your classic Peruvian ceviche immediately, preferably chilled. Serve with toasted corn kernels (cancha) or plantain chips on the side for added crunch.

Mixed Seafood Ceviche

Ingredients:

- 1/2 lb fresh white fish fillets (such as sea bass, tilapia, or sole), diced into bite-sized pieces
- 1/2 lb shrimp, peeled, deveined, and chopped
- 1/2 lb scallops, chopped
- 1 cup freshly squeezed lime juice
- 1 red onion, thinly sliced
- 1-2 hot peppers (aji amarillo or jalapeño), seeded and finely chopped
- 1-2 cloves garlic, minced
- 1/4 cup chopped cilantro
- 1-2 tomatoes, seeded and diced
- Salt, to taste
- Pepper, to taste
- Corn kernels (optional)
- Sweet potato, boiled and sliced (optional)
- Lettuce leaves (for serving)

Instructions:

In a large glass or ceramic bowl, combine the diced fish, chopped shrimp, and chopped scallops with the lime juice. Make sure all the seafood is completely submerged in the lime juice. Cover the bowl with plastic wrap and refrigerate for about 20-30 minutes. The seafood should become opaque and "cooked" in the lime juice.

While the seafood is marinating, prepare the other ingredients. Thinly slice the red onion, finely chop the hot peppers, mince the garlic, chop the cilantro, and dice the tomatoes.

After the seafood has marinated, drain off most of the lime juice, leaving just a little to keep the ceviche moist. Add the sliced red onion, chopped hot peppers, minced garlic, chopped cilantro, and diced tomatoes to the bowl with the seafood.

Season the ceviche with salt and pepper, to taste. Gently toss all the ingredients together until well combined.

If desired, add corn kernels and sliced boiled sweet potato to the ceviche for extra flavor and texture.

To serve, line a serving platter or individual plates with lettuce leaves. Spoon the mixed seafood ceviche onto the lettuce leaves and garnish with additional cilantro leaves, if desired.

Enjoy your mixed seafood ceviche immediately, preferably chilled. Serve with toasted corn kernels (cancha) or plantain chips on the side for added crunch.

Fisherman's Ceviche

Ingredients:

- 1 lb fresh white fish fillets (such as sea bass, tilapia, or sole), diced into bite-sized pieces
- 1/2 lb shrimp, peeled, deveined, and chopped
- 1/2 lb squid, cleaned and sliced into rings
- 1 cup freshly squeezed lime juice
- 1 red onion, thinly sliced
- 1-2 hot peppers (aji amarillo or jalapeño), seeded and finely chopped
- 1-2 cloves garlic, minced
- 1/4 cup chopped cilantro
- 1-2 tomatoes, seeded and diced
- Salt, to taste
- Pepper, to taste
- Corn kernels (optional)
- Sweet potato, boiled and sliced (optional)
- Lettuce leaves (for serving)

Instructions:

In a large glass or ceramic bowl, combine the diced fish, chopped shrimp, and sliced squid with the lime juice. Make sure all the seafood is completely submerged in the lime juice. Cover the bowl with plastic wrap and refrigerate for about 20-30 minutes. The seafood should become opaque and "cooked" in the lime juice.

While the seafood is marinating, prepare the other ingredients. Thinly slice the red onion, finely chop the hot peppers, mince the garlic, chop the cilantro, and dice the tomatoes.

After the seafood has marinated, drain off most of the lime juice, leaving just a little to keep the ceviche moist. Add the sliced red onion, chopped hot peppers, minced garlic, chopped cilantro, and diced tomatoes to the bowl with the seafood.

Season the ceviche with salt and pepper, to taste. Gently toss all the ingredients together until well combined.

If desired, add corn kernels and sliced boiled sweet potato to the ceviche for extra flavor and texture.

To serve, line a serving platter or individual plates with lettuce leaves. Spoon the Fisherman's ceviche onto the lettuce leaves and garnish with additional cilantro leaves, if desired.

Enjoy your Fisherman's ceviche immediately, preferably chilled. Serve with toasted corn kernels (cancha) or plantain chips on the side for added crunch.

Scallop and Shrimp Ceviche

Ingredients:

- 1/2 lb fresh scallops, muscle removed and thinly sliced
- 1/2 lb shrimp, peeled, deveined, and chopped
- 1 cup freshly squeezed lime juice
- 1 red onion, thinly sliced
- 1-2 hot peppers (aji amarillo or jalapeño), seeded and finely chopped
- 1-2 cloves garlic, minced
- 1/4 cup chopped cilantro
- 1-2 tomatoes, seeded and diced
- Salt, to taste
- Pepper, to taste
- Corn kernels (optional)
- Sweet potato, boiled and sliced (optional)
- Lettuce leaves (for serving)

Instructions:

In a large glass or ceramic bowl, combine the sliced scallops and chopped shrimp with the lime juice. Make sure all the seafood is completely submerged in the lime juice. Cover the bowl with plastic wrap and refrigerate for about 20-30 minutes. The seafood should become opaque and "cooked" in the lime juice. While the seafood is marinating, prepare the other ingredients. Thinly slice the red onion, finely chop the hot peppers, mince the garlic, chop the cilantro, and dice the tomatoes.

After the seafood has marinated, drain off most of the lime juice, leaving just a little to keep the ceviche moist. Add the sliced red onion, chopped hot peppers, minced garlic, chopped cilantro, and diced tomatoes to the bowl with the seafood.

Season the ceviche with salt and pepper, to taste. Gently toss all the ingredients together until well combined.

If desired, add corn kernels and sliced boiled sweet potato to the ceviche for extra flavor and texture.

To serve, line a serving platter or individual plates with lettuce leaves. Spoon the Scallop and Shrimp ceviche onto the lettuce leaves and garnish with additional cilantro leaves, if desired.

Enjoy your Scallop and Shrimp ceviche immediately, preferably chilled. Serve with toasted corn kernels (cancha) or plantain chips on the side for added crunch.

Octopus Ceviche

Ingredients:

- 1 lb octopus, cleaned and tentacles chopped into bite-sized pieces
- 1 cup freshly squeezed lime juice
- 1 red onion, thinly sliced
- 1-2 hot peppers (aji amarillo or jalapeño), seeded and finely chopped
- 1-2 cloves garlic, minced
- 1/4 cup chopped cilantro
- 1-2 tomatoes, seeded and diced
- Salt, to taste
- Pepper, to taste
- Corn kernels (optional)
- Sweet potato, boiled and sliced (optional)
- Lettuce leaves (for serving)

Instructions:

In a large glass or ceramic bowl, combine the chopped octopus with the lime juice. Make sure the octopus is completely submerged in the lime juice. Cover the bowl with plastic wrap and refrigerate for about 20-30 minutes. The octopus should become tender and opaque in the lime juice.
While the octopus is marinating, prepare the other ingredients. Thinly slice the red onion, finely chop the hot peppers, mince the garlic, chop the cilantro, and dice the tomatoes.
After the octopus has marinated, drain off most of the lime juice, leaving just a little to keep the ceviche moist. Add the sliced red onion, chopped hot peppers, minced garlic, chopped cilantro, and diced tomatoes to the bowl with the octopus.
Season the ceviche with salt and pepper, to taste. Gently toss all the ingredients together until well combined.
If desired, add corn kernels and sliced boiled sweet potato to the ceviche for extra flavor and texture.
To serve, line a serving platter or individual plates with lettuce leaves. Spoon the Octopus ceviche onto the lettuce leaves and garnish with additional cilantro leaves, if desired.

Enjoy your Octopus ceviche immediately, preferably chilled. Serve with toasted corn kernels (cancha) or plantain chips on the side for added crunch.

Spicy Tuna Ceviche

Ingredients:

- 1 lb sushi-grade tuna, diced into bite-sized pieces
- 1/4 cup soy sauce
- 2 tablespoons rice vinegar
- 1 tablespoon sesame oil
- 1 tablespoon sriracha sauce (adjust according to spice preference)
- 1 teaspoon grated ginger
- 1 teaspoon minced garlic
- 1/4 cup chopped green onions
- 1/4 cup chopped cilantro
- 1 avocado, diced
- 1 jalapeño pepper, thinly sliced
- 1 lime, juiced
- Salt, to taste
- Pepper, to taste
- Sesame seeds, for garnish
- Tortilla chips or crackers, for serving

Instructions:

In a large mixing bowl, combine the soy sauce, rice vinegar, sesame oil, sriracha sauce, grated ginger, and minced garlic. Whisk together until well combined to make the marinade.

Add the diced tuna to the marinade and toss until the tuna is evenly coated.

Cover the bowl with plastic wrap and refrigerate for about 20-30 minutes to allow the flavors to meld.

While the tuna is marinating, prepare the other ingredients. Chop the green onions, cilantro, avocado, and jalapeño pepper. Juice the lime.

After the tuna has marinated, remove it from the refrigerator. Add the chopped green onions, cilantro, avocado, and jalapeño pepper to the bowl with the tuna. Squeeze the lime juice over the mixture.

Season the ceviche with salt and pepper, to taste. Gently toss all the ingredients together until well combined.

To serve, transfer the Spicy Tuna Ceviche to a serving dish. Garnish with sesame seeds for extra flavor and texture.

Serve the Spicy Tuna Ceviche immediately with tortilla chips or crackers on the side for scooping.

Enjoy your Spicy Tuna Ceviche as a refreshing and flavorful appetizer or light meal!

Mango and Avocado Ceviche

Ingredients:

- 1 ripe mango, diced
- 1 ripe avocado, diced
- 1/2 red onion, finely chopped
- 1-2 jalapeño peppers, seeded and finely chopped
- 1/4 cup chopped cilantro
- Juice of 2-3 limes
- Salt, to taste
- Pepper, to taste
- Tortilla chips or crackers, for serving

Instructions:

In a large mixing bowl, combine the diced mango, diced avocado, chopped red onion, chopped jalapeño peppers, and chopped cilantro.
Squeeze the lime juice over the mixture. Start with the juice of 2 limes and adjust according to taste preference.
Season the ceviche with salt and pepper, to taste. Gently toss all the ingredients together until well combined.
Cover the bowl with plastic wrap and refrigerate for about 15-20 minutes to allow the flavors to meld together.
After chilling, give the ceviche a final toss to ensure all ingredients are evenly coated with lime juice and seasoning.
To serve, transfer the Mango and Avocado Ceviche to a serving dish. Garnish with additional cilantro leaves or lime wedges, if desired.
Serve the Mango and Avocado Ceviche immediately with tortilla chips or crackers on the side for scooping.
Enjoy this refreshing and tropical twist on ceviche as a flavorful appetizer or light snack!

Coconut Milk Ceviche

Ingredients:

- 1 lb fresh white fish fillets (such as sea bass, tilapia, or sole), diced into bite-sized pieces
- 1 cup coconut milk
- 1 red onion, thinly sliced
- 1-2 hot peppers (aji amarillo or jalapeño), seeded and finely chopped
- 1-2 cloves garlic, minced
- 1/4 cup chopped cilantro
- 1-2 tomatoes, seeded and diced
- Juice of 2-3 limes
- Salt, to taste
- Pepper, to taste
- Toasted coconut flakes (optional, for garnish)
- Tortilla chips or crackers, for serving

Instructions:

In a large mixing bowl, combine the diced fish, sliced red onion, chopped hot peppers, minced garlic, chopped cilantro, and diced tomatoes.

Pour the coconut milk over the mixture and squeeze the lime juice over it as well. Start with the juice of 2 limes and adjust according to taste preference.

Season the ceviche with salt and pepper, to taste. Gently toss all the ingredients together until well combined.

Cover the bowl with plastic wrap and refrigerate for about 20-30 minutes to allow the flavors to meld together.

After chilling, give the ceviche a final toss to ensure all ingredients are evenly coated with coconut milk, lime juice, and seasoning.

To serve, transfer the Coconut Milk Ceviche to a serving dish. Garnish with toasted coconut flakes for an extra tropical touch, if desired.

Serve the Coconut Milk Ceviche immediately with tortilla chips or crackers on the side for scooping.

Enjoy this creamy and refreshing Coconut Milk Ceviche as a delightful appetizer or light meal with a taste of the tropics!

Ceviche Tostadas

Ingredients:

- 1 lb fresh white fish fillets (such as sea bass, tilapia, or sole), diced into bite-sized pieces
- 1 red onion, finely chopped
- 1-2 hot peppers (aji amarillo or jalapeño), seeded and finely chopped
- 1-2 cloves garlic, minced
- 1/4 cup chopped cilantro
- 1-2 tomatoes, seeded and diced
- Juice of 2-3 limes
- Salt, to taste
- Pepper, to taste
- 8 tostada shells
- Avocado slices, for garnish
- Lime wedges, for garnish

Instructions:

In a large mixing bowl, combine the diced fish, chopped red onion, chopped hot peppers, minced garlic, chopped cilantro, and diced tomatoes.
Squeeze the lime juice over the mixture. Start with the juice of 2 limes and adjust according to taste preference.
Season the ceviche with salt and pepper, to taste. Gently toss all the ingredients together until well combined.
Cover the bowl with plastic wrap and refrigerate for about 20-30 minutes to allow the flavors to meld together.
While the ceviche is marinating, prepare the tostada shells according to package instructions, or you can use store-bought tostadas.
Once the ceviche is ready, spoon a generous amount of the mixture onto each tostada shell.
Garnish each tostada with slices of avocado and additional cilantro leaves, if desired.
Serve the Ceviche Tostadas immediately with lime wedges on the side for squeezing.
Enjoy these flavorful and crunchy Ceviche Tostadas as a delicious appetizer or light meal!

Ceviche Tacos

Ingredients:

For the Ceviche:

- 1 lb fresh white fish fillets (such as sea bass, tilapia, or sole), diced into bite-sized pieces
- 1 red onion, finely chopped
- 1-2 hot peppers (aji amarillo or jalapeño), seeded and finely chopped
- 1-2 cloves garlic, minced
- 1/4 cup chopped cilantro
- 1-2 tomatoes, seeded and diced
- Juice of 2-3 limes
- Salt, to taste
- Pepper, to taste

For the Tacos:

- 8 small corn or flour tortillas
- 1 avocado, sliced
- Lime wedges, for serving
- Additional chopped cilantro, for garnish
- Hot sauce or salsa, optional

Instructions:

In a large mixing bowl, combine the diced fish, chopped red onion, chopped hot peppers, minced garlic, chopped cilantro, and diced tomatoes.

Squeeze the lime juice over the mixture. Start with the juice of 2 limes and adjust according to taste preference.

Season the ceviche with salt and pepper, to taste. Gently toss all the ingredients together until well combined.

Cover the bowl with plastic wrap and refrigerate for about 20-30 minutes to allow the flavors to meld together.

While the ceviche is marinating, warm the tortillas in a dry skillet or oven until soft and pliable.

Once the ceviche is ready, spoon a generous amount of the mixture onto each tortilla.

Top each ceviche-filled tortilla with slices of avocado and a sprinkle of additional chopped cilantro.

Serve the Ceviche Tacos immediately with lime wedges on the side for squeezing. Optionally, offer hot sauce or salsa for extra flavor.

Enjoy these delicious and refreshing Ceviche Tacos as a tasty meal or appetizer!

Ceviche Stuffed Avocado

Ingredients:

- 1 lb fresh white fish fillets (such as sea bass, tilapia, or sole), diced into bite-sized pieces
- 1 red onion, finely chopped
- 1-2 hot peppers (aji amarillo or jalapeño), seeded and finely chopped
- 1-2 cloves garlic, minced
- 1/4 cup chopped cilantro
- 1-2 tomatoes, seeded and diced
- Juice of 2-3 limes
- Salt, to taste
- Pepper, to taste
- 4 ripe avocados, halved and pitted

Instructions:

In a large mixing bowl, combine the diced fish, chopped red onion, chopped hot peppers, minced garlic, chopped cilantro, and diced tomatoes.

Squeeze the lime juice over the mixture. Start with the juice of 2 limes and adjust according to taste preference.

Season the ceviche with salt and pepper, to taste. Gently toss all the ingredients together until well combined.

Cover the bowl with plastic wrap and refrigerate for about 20-30 minutes to allow the flavors to meld together.

While the ceviche is marinating, prepare the avocados. Halve the avocados and remove the pits. Use a spoon to scoop out a little extra flesh from each half to create a cavity for the ceviche.

Once the ceviche is ready, spoon a generous amount of the mixture into each avocado half, filling the cavity.

Garnish each ceviche-stuffed avocado half with additional chopped cilantro.

Serve the Ceviche Stuffed Avocado immediately as a refreshing and flavorful appetizer or light meal.

Enjoy this unique and delicious dish that combines the creaminess of avocado with the tangy flavors of ceviche!

Ceviche Lettuce Wraps

Ingredients:

- 1 lb fresh white fish fillets (such as sea bass, tilapia, or sole), diced into bite-sized pieces
- 1 red onion, finely chopped
- 1-2 hot peppers (aji amarillo or jalapeño), seeded and finely chopped
- 1-2 cloves garlic, minced
- 1/4 cup chopped cilantro
- 1-2 tomatoes, seeded and diced
- Juice of 2-3 limes
- Salt, to taste
- Pepper, to taste
- 1 head of iceberg or butter lettuce, leaves separated and washed

Instructions:

In a large mixing bowl, combine the diced fish, chopped red onion, chopped hot peppers, minced garlic, chopped cilantro, and diced tomatoes.
Squeeze the lime juice over the mixture. Start with the juice of 2 limes and adjust according to taste preference.
Season the ceviche with salt and pepper, to taste. Gently toss all the ingredients together until well combined.
Cover the bowl with plastic wrap and refrigerate for about 20-30 minutes to allow the flavors to meld together.
Once the ceviche is ready, spoon a generous amount of the mixture onto each lettuce leaf.
Serve the Ceviche Lettuce Wraps immediately as a refreshing and light appetizer or meal.
Enjoy the crisp and refreshing combination of lettuce with tangy ceviche flavors!

Ceviche Stuffed Mini Peppers

Ingredients:

- 1 lb fresh white fish fillets (such as sea bass, tilapia, or sole), diced into bite-sized pieces
- 1 red onion, finely chopped
- 1-2 hot peppers (aji amarillo or jalapeño), seeded and finely chopped
- 1-2 cloves garlic, minced
- 1/4 cup chopped cilantro
- 1-2 tomatoes, seeded and diced
- Juice of 2-3 limes
- Salt, to taste
- Pepper, to taste
- Mini sweet peppers, halved and seeded

Instructions:

In a large mixing bowl, combine the diced fish, chopped red onion, chopped hot peppers, minced garlic, chopped cilantro, and diced tomatoes.

Squeeze the lime juice over the mixture. Start with the juice of 2 limes and adjust according to taste preference.

Season the ceviche with salt and pepper, to taste. Gently toss all the ingredients together until well combined.

Cover the bowl with plastic wrap and refrigerate for about 20-30 minutes to allow the flavors to meld together.

While the ceviche is marinating, prepare the mini sweet peppers. Cut each pepper in half lengthwise and remove the seeds and membranes.

Once the ceviche is ready, spoon a generous amount of the mixture into each mini pepper half.

Arrange the stuffed mini peppers on a serving platter.

Serve the Ceviche Stuffed Mini Peppers immediately as a flavorful and colorful appetizer or light snack.

Enjoy the vibrant flavors of ceviche paired with the sweetness of the mini peppers!

Ceviche Rice Bowls

Ingredients:

For the Ceviche:

- 1 lb fresh white fish fillets (such as sea bass, tilapia, or sole), diced into bite-sized pieces
- 1 red onion, finely chopped
- 1-2 hot peppers (aji amarillo or jalapeño), seeded and finely chopped
- 1-2 cloves garlic, minced
- 1/4 cup chopped cilantro
- 1-2 tomatoes, seeded and diced
- Juice of 2-3 limes
- Salt, to taste
- Pepper, to taste

For the Rice Bowls:

- Cooked white or brown rice
- Avocado slices
- Lime wedges
- Additional chopped cilantro, for garnish
- Optional toppings: sliced radishes, diced mango, shredded lettuce, black beans, corn kernels, sliced jalapeños, sour cream, hot sauce

Instructions:

In a large mixing bowl, combine the diced fish, chopped red onion, chopped hot peppers, minced garlic, chopped cilantro, and diced tomatoes.
Squeeze the lime juice over the mixture. Start with the juice of 2 limes and adjust according to taste preference.
Season the ceviche with salt and pepper, to taste. Gently toss all the ingredients together until well combined.
Cover the bowl with plastic wrap and refrigerate for about 20-30 minutes to allow the flavors to meld together.

While the ceviche is marinating, prepare the rice according to package instructions.

Once the ceviche is ready, assemble the rice bowls. Divide the cooked rice among serving bowls.

Top each rice bowl with a generous portion of the ceviche mixture.

Add avocado slices and additional chopped cilantro on top of the ceviche.

Serve the Ceviche Rice Bowls with lime wedges on the side for squeezing.

Optionally, offer additional toppings such as sliced radishes, diced mango, shredded lettuce, black beans, corn kernels, sliced jalapeños, sour cream, or hot sauce for customization.

Enjoy these flavorful and customizable Ceviche Rice Bowls as a delicious and satisfying meal!

Ceviche Salad

Ingredients:

For the Ceviche:

- 1 lb fresh white fish fillets (such as sea bass, tilapia, or sole), diced into bite-sized pieces
- 1 red onion, finely chopped
- 1-2 hot peppers (aji amarillo or jalapeño), seeded and finely chopped
- 1-2 cloves garlic, minced
- 1/4 cup chopped cilantro
- 1-2 tomatoes, seeded and diced
- Juice of 2-3 limes
- Salt, to taste
- Pepper, to taste

For the Salad:

- Mixed salad greens (such as lettuce, spinach, or arugula)
- Cherry tomatoes, halved
- Cucumber, sliced
- Avocado, sliced
- Radishes, thinly sliced
- Red bell pepper, thinly sliced
- Optional toppings: sliced jalapeños, corn kernels, black beans, sliced olives

Instructions:

In a large mixing bowl, combine the diced fish, chopped red onion, chopped hot peppers, minced garlic, chopped cilantro, and diced tomatoes.
Squeeze the lime juice over the mixture. Start with the juice of 2 limes and adjust according to taste preference.
Season the ceviche with salt and pepper, to taste. Gently toss all the ingredients together until well combined.
Cover the bowl with plastic wrap and refrigerate for about 20-30 minutes to allow the flavors to meld together.

While the ceviche is marinating, prepare the salad ingredients. Wash and dry the salad greens, halve the cherry tomatoes, slice the cucumber, avocado, and radishes, and thinly slice the red bell pepper.

Once the ceviche is ready, assemble the salad. Place the mixed salad greens in a large serving bowl or on individual plates.

Top the salad greens with the ceviche mixture.

Arrange the cherry tomatoes, cucumber slices, avocado slices, radish slices, and red bell pepper slices around the ceviche.

Optionally, add additional toppings such as sliced jalapeños, corn kernels, black beans, or sliced olives.

Serve the Ceviche Salad immediately, optionally drizzling with additional lime juice or olive oil.

Enjoy this refreshing and flavorful Ceviche Salad as a light and satisfying meal!

Passion Fruit Ceviche

Ingredients:

- 1 lb fresh white fish fillets (such as sea bass, tilapia, or sole), diced into bite-sized pieces
- 1 red onion, finely chopped
- 1-2 hot peppers (aji amarillo or jalapeño), seeded and finely chopped
- 1-2 cloves garlic, minced
- 1/4 cup chopped cilantro
- 1-2 tomatoes, seeded and diced
- Juice of 2-3 limes
- Juice of 2-3 passion fruits
- Salt, to taste
- Pepper, to taste
- Optional: chopped mango, diced avocado, sliced radishes, sliced cucumber

Instructions:

In a large mixing bowl, combine the diced fish, chopped red onion, chopped hot peppers, minced garlic, chopped cilantro, and diced tomatoes.
In a separate bowl, whisk together the lime juice and passion fruit juice.
Pour the lime and passion fruit juice mixture over the fish mixture.
Season the ceviche with salt and pepper, to taste. Gently toss all the ingredients together until well combined.
Cover the bowl with plastic wrap and refrigerate for about 20-30 minutes to allow the flavors to meld together.
While the ceviche is marinating, prepare any optional ingredients such as chopped mango, diced avocado, sliced radishes, or sliced cucumber.
Once the ceviche is ready, serve it chilled, garnished with additional cilantro if desired. Optionally, serve with tortilla chips or crackers on the side.
Enjoy this unique and tropical twist on ceviche with the delightful flavor of passion fruit!

Quinoa Ceviche Salad

Ingredients:

For the Ceviche:

- 1 lb fresh white fish fillets (such as sea bass, tilapia, or sole), diced into bite-sized pieces
- 1 red onion, finely chopped
- 1-2 hot peppers (aji amarillo or jalapeño), seeded and finely chopped
- 1-2 cloves garlic, minced
- 1/4 cup chopped cilantro
- 1-2 tomatoes, seeded and diced
- Juice of 2-3 limes
- Salt, to taste
- Pepper, to taste

For the Quinoa:

- 1 cup quinoa, rinsed
- 2 cups water or vegetable broth
- Salt, to taste

For the Salad:

- Cooked quinoa
- Ceviche mixture
- Mixed salad greens (such as lettuce, spinach, or arugula)
- Avocado, diced
- Cucumber, diced
- Radishes, thinly sliced
- Red bell pepper, diced
- Optional toppings: sliced jalapeños, corn kernels, black beans, sliced olives

Instructions:

Cook the quinoa according to package instructions. In a medium saucepan, combine the rinsed quinoa with water or vegetable broth and a pinch of salt. Bring to a boil, then reduce heat to low, cover, and simmer for about 15-20 minutes, or until the quinoa is cooked and water is absorbed. Fluff with a fork and let it cool slightly.

In a large mixing bowl, combine the diced fish, chopped red onion, chopped hot peppers, minced garlic, chopped cilantro, and diced tomatoes.

Squeeze the lime juice over the mixture. Start with the juice of 2 limes and adjust according to taste preference.

Season the ceviche with salt and pepper, to taste. Gently toss all the ingredients together until well combined.

Cover the bowl with plastic wrap and refrigerate for about 20-30 minutes to allow the flavors to meld together.

Once the quinoa and ceviche are ready, assemble the salad. In a large serving bowl or on individual plates, layer the cooked quinoa, mixed salad greens, and ceviche mixture.

Top the salad with diced avocado, diced cucumber, thinly sliced radishes, and diced red bell pepper.

Optionally, add additional toppings such as sliced jalapeños, corn kernels, black beans, or sliced olives.

Serve the Quinoa Ceviche Salad immediately, optionally drizzling with additional lime juice or olive oil.

Enjoy this nutritious and flavorful salad as a satisfying meal!

Peruvian Ceviche Soup

Ingredients:

- 1 lb fresh white fish fillets (such as sea bass, tilapia, or sole), diced into bite-sized pieces
- 4 cups fish or vegetable broth
- 1 red onion, thinly sliced
- 1-2 hot peppers (aji amarillo or jalapeño), seeded and finely chopped
- 2-3 cloves garlic, minced
- 1/4 cup chopped cilantro
- 1-2 tomatoes, seeded and diced
- Juice of 4-5 limes
- Salt, to taste
- Pepper, to taste
- Corn kernels (fresh or frozen), cooked
- Sweet potato, boiled and sliced
- Lettuce leaves, shredded
- Corn nuts or toasted corn kernels (cancha), for garnish
- Optional: sliced avocado, sliced boiled eggs, chopped parsley

Instructions:

In a large pot, bring the fish or vegetable broth to a gentle simmer over medium heat.

Once the broth is simmering, add the diced fish to the pot. Let it cook for about 2-3 minutes until the fish is opaque and cooked through. Remove the fish from the broth using a slotted spoon and set it aside in a bowl.

In the same pot with the broth, add the thinly sliced red onion, chopped hot peppers, minced garlic, chopped cilantro, and diced tomatoes. Let the vegetables simmer in the broth for about 5 minutes until they are softened.

Turn off the heat and add the cooked fish back into the pot with the vegetables. Squeeze the lime juice over the ceviche soup mixture. Start with the juice of 4 limes and adjust according to taste preference.

Season the ceviche soup with salt and pepper, to taste. Stir well to combine all the ingredients.

To serve, ladle the Peruvian Ceviche Soup into bowls. Garnish each bowl with cooked corn kernels, sliced boiled sweet potato, shredded lettuce, and corn nuts or toasted corn kernels.

Optionally, add sliced avocado, sliced boiled eggs, or chopped parsley as additional garnishes.

Serve the Peruvian Ceviche Soup immediately, allowing guests to customize their bowls with additional lime juice or hot sauce if desired.

Enjoy this flavorful and refreshing Peruvian Ceviche Soup as a unique and satisfying dish!

Peruvian Ceviche Pizza

Ingredients:

For the Pizza Dough:

- 1 pound (about 3 1/4 cups) bread flour, plus more for dusting
- 2 teaspoons instant yeast
- 1 teaspoon salt
- 1 tablespoon sugar
- 2 tablespoons olive oil
- 1 cup warm water

For the Ceviche Topping:

- 1 lb fresh white fish fillets (such as sea bass, tilapia, or sole), diced into small pieces
- Juice of 4-5 limes
- 1 red onion, finely chopped
- 1-2 hot peppers (aji amarillo or jalapeño), seeded and finely chopped
- 2-3 cloves garlic, minced
- 1/4 cup chopped cilantro
- 1-2 tomatoes, seeded and diced
- Salt, to taste
- Pepper, to taste

For Assembling the Pizza:

- Olive oil, for brushing
- Cornmeal, for dusting
- Sliced red onions
- Sliced jalapeños
- Sliced avocado
- Lime wedges
- Additional cilantro, for garnish
- Hot sauce, for serving (optional)

Instructions:

Prepare the Pizza Dough:
- In a large mixing bowl, combine the bread flour, instant yeast, salt, and sugar. Stir to combine.
- Make a well in the center of the dry ingredients and add the olive oil and warm water.
- Use a wooden spoon or your hands to mix until a dough forms.
- Transfer the dough to a lightly floured surface and knead for about 5-7 minutes until smooth and elastic.
- Place the dough in a lightly oiled bowl, cover with plastic wrap, and let it rise in a warm place for about 1 hour or until doubled in size.

Prepare the Ceviche Topping:
- In a large mixing bowl, combine the diced fish with the lime juice. Let it marinate for about 10-15 minutes until the fish turns opaque.
- Add the finely chopped red onion, hot peppers, minced garlic, chopped cilantro, and diced tomatoes to the fish mixture.
- Season with salt and pepper to taste. Stir well to combine all the ingredients. Set aside.

Preheat the oven to 475°F (245°C). If you have a pizza stone, place it in the oven to preheat as well.

Assemble the Pizza:
- Once the dough has risen, punch it down and divide it into two equal portions. Roll out each portion of dough on a lightly floured surface into a circle or rectangle, depending on your preference for pizza shape.
- Transfer the rolled-out dough to a baking sheet or pizza peel dusted with cornmeal.
- Brush the edges of the dough with olive oil.
- Spread a generous amount of the ceviche mixture evenly over the dough, leaving a small border around the edges.
- Top the ceviche with sliced red onions and jalapeños.
- Carefully transfer the pizza to the preheated oven (either directly onto the pizza stone or onto the baking sheet) and bake for 12-15 minutes or until the crust is golden brown and crisp.

Once the pizza is done, remove it from the oven and let it cool slightly. Top with sliced avocado, fresh cilantro, and lime wedges.

Serve the Peruvian Ceviche Pizza immediately, slicing it into portions and offering hot sauce on the side for those who desire an extra kick.

Enjoy this unique and flavorful fusion dish that brings together the best of both ceviche and pizza!

Peruvian Ceviche Spring Rolls

Ingredients:

For the Ceviche Filling:

- 1 lb fresh white fish fillets (such as sea bass, tilapia, or sole), diced into small pieces
- Juice of 4-5 limes
- 1 red onion, finely chopped
- 1-2 hot peppers (aji amarillo or jalapeño), seeded and finely chopped
- 2-3 cloves garlic, minced
- 1/4 cup chopped cilantro
- 1-2 tomatoes, seeded and diced
- Salt, to taste
- Pepper, to taste

For the Spring Rolls:

- Rice paper wrappers (spring roll wrappers)
- Lettuce leaves
- Thinly sliced cucumber
- Thinly sliced avocado
- Thinly sliced radishes
- Fresh cilantro leaves
- Lime wedges
- Sweet chili sauce or soy sauce, for dipping (optional)

Instructions:

Prepare the Ceviche Filling:
- In a large mixing bowl, combine the diced fish with the lime juice. Let it marinate for about 10-15 minutes until the fish turns opaque.
- Add the finely chopped red onion, hot peppers, minced garlic, chopped cilantro, and diced tomatoes to the fish mixture.
- Season with salt and pepper to taste. Stir well to combine all the ingredients. Set aside.

Prepare the Spring Rolls:
- Fill a shallow dish or large bowl with warm water.
- Dip one rice paper wrapper into the warm water for about 5-10 seconds, or until it becomes soft and pliable.
- Carefully remove the softened rice paper wrapper from the water and lay it flat on a clean work surface, such as a cutting board or plate.

Assemble the Spring Rolls:
- Place a lettuce leaf in the center of the rice paper wrapper.
- Add a spoonful of the ceviche filling on top of the lettuce leaf.
- Top the ceviche filling with thinly sliced cucumber, avocado, and radishes.
- Sprinkle fresh cilantro leaves over the filling.
- Fold the bottom edge of the rice paper wrapper over the filling, then fold in the sides, and roll it up tightly into a spring roll.
- Repeat the process with the remaining rice paper wrappers and filling ingredients.

Serve the Peruvian Ceviche Spring Rolls immediately, with lime wedges on the side for squeezing and sweet chili sauce or soy sauce for dipping, if desired. Enjoy these refreshing and flavorful Peruvian Ceviche Spring Rolls as a unique appetizer or light meal!

Peruvian Ceviche Empanadas

Ingredients:

For the Ceviche Filling:

- 1 lb fresh white fish fillets (such as sea bass, tilapia, or sole), diced into small pieces
- Juice of 4-5 limes
- 1 red onion, finely chopped
- 1-2 hot peppers (aji amarillo or jalapeño), seeded and finely chopped
- 2-3 cloves garlic, minced
- 1/4 cup chopped cilantro
- 1-2 tomatoes, seeded and diced
- Salt, to taste
- Pepper, to taste

For the Empanada Dough:

- 3 cups all-purpose flour, plus extra for dusting
- 1 teaspoon salt
- 1 cup unsalted butter, cold and diced
- 1/2 cup ice-cold water

For Assembly:

- Egg wash (1 egg beaten with 1 tablespoon water)
- Lime wedges, for serving
- Hot sauce or salsa, for dipping (optional)

Instructions:

Prepare the Ceviche Filling:
- In a large mixing bowl, combine the diced fish with the lime juice. Let it marinate for about 10-15 minutes until the fish turns opaque.
- Add the finely chopped red onion, hot peppers, minced garlic, chopped cilantro, and diced tomatoes to the fish mixture.

- Season with salt and pepper to taste. Stir well to combine all the ingredients. Set aside.

Prepare the Empanada Dough:
- In a large mixing bowl, whisk together the flour and salt.
- Add the cold diced butter to the flour mixture and use your fingers or a pastry cutter to cut the butter into the flour until the mixture resembles coarse crumbs.
- Gradually add the ice-cold water, a little at a time, mixing until a dough forms. Be careful not to overwork the dough.
- Shape the dough into a ball, wrap it in plastic wrap, and refrigerate for at least 30 minutes to chill.

Preheat the oven to 375°F (190°C). Line a baking sheet with parchment paper.

Roll out the Empanada Dough:
- On a lightly floured surface, roll out the chilled dough to about 1/8 inch thickness.
- Use a round cutter or a small plate to cut out circles from the dough, each about 4-5 inches in diameter.

Assemble the Empanadas:
- Place a spoonful of the ceviche filling in the center of each dough circle.
- Brush the edges of the dough circles with egg wash.
- Fold the dough over the filling to create a half-moon shape and press the edges together to seal.
- Use a fork to crimp the edges of the empanadas for a decorative touch.

Place the assembled empanadas on the prepared baking sheet. Brush the tops with egg wash.

Bake the Empanadas:
- Bake the empanadas in the preheated oven for about 20-25 minutes or until golden brown and crispy.

Serve the Peruvian Ceviche Empanadas hot or at room temperature, with lime wedges and hot sauce or salsa on the side for dipping.

Enjoy these flavorful and satisfying Peruvian Ceviche Empanadas as a tasty appetizer or snack!

Peruvian Ceviche Sushi Rolls

Ingredients:

For the Ceviche Filling:

- 1 lb fresh white fish fillets (such as sea bass, tilapia, or sole), diced into small pieces
- Juice of 4-5 limes
- 1 red onion, finely chopped
- 1-2 hot peppers (aji amarillo or jalapeño), seeded and finely chopped
- 2-3 cloves garlic, minced
- 1/4 cup chopped cilantro
- 1-2 tomatoes, seeded and diced
- Salt, to taste
- Pepper, to taste

For the Sushi Rice:

- 2 cups sushi rice
- 2 1/2 cups water
- 1/3 cup rice vinegar
- 2 tablespoons sugar
- 1 teaspoon salt

For Assembly:

- Nori seaweed sheets
- Sushi rolling mat (makisu)
- Sliced avocado
- Sliced cucumber
- Sliced mango
- Thinly sliced jalapeño (optional)
- Soy sauce, for dipping
- Pickled ginger, for serving
- Wasabi, for serving

Instructions:

Prepare the Ceviche Filling:
- In a large mixing bowl, combine the diced fish with the lime juice. Let it marinate for about 10-15 minutes until the fish turns opaque.
- Add the finely chopped red onion, hot peppers, minced garlic, chopped cilantro, and diced tomatoes to the fish mixture.
- Season with salt and pepper to taste. Stir well to combine all the ingredients. Set aside.

Prepare the Sushi Rice:
- Rinse the sushi rice under cold water until the water runs clear.
- In a rice cooker or saucepan, combine the rinsed rice and water. Cook according to the rice cooker instructions or bring to a boil, then reduce the heat to low, cover, and simmer for about 18-20 minutes until the rice is cooked and the water is absorbed.
- In a small saucepan, heat the rice vinegar, sugar, and salt over low heat until the sugar and salt are dissolved. Remove from heat and let it cool.
- Once the rice is cooked, transfer it to a large mixing bowl and gently fold in the seasoned rice vinegar mixture until well combined. Let the rice cool to room temperature.

Assemble the Sushi Rolls:
- Place a sheet of nori seaweed shiny side down on a sushi rolling mat.
- With damp hands, spread a thin layer of sushi rice evenly over the nori, leaving about 1 inch of space at the top edge.
- Arrange a line of ceviche filling, sliced avocado, cucumber, mango, and jalapeño (if using) horizontally across the center of the rice.
- Using the sushi rolling mat, carefully roll the nori and rice over the filling, tucking the ingredients tightly as you roll.
- Continue rolling until the entire sheet of nori is rolled up into a tight cylinder.
- Wet the exposed edge of the nori with a bit of water to seal the roll.
- Repeat the process with the remaining nori sheets and filling ingredients.

Slice the Sushi Rolls:
- Use a sharp knife to slice the sushi roll into individual pieces, about 1 inch thick. Wipe the knife clean between slices for clean cuts.

Serve the Peruvian Ceviche Sushi Rolls:
- Arrange the sliced sushi rolls on a serving platter.
- Serve with soy sauce, pickled ginger, and wasabi on the side for dipping.

Enjoy these unique and flavorful Peruvian Ceviche Sushi Rolls as a stunning appetizer or light meal!

Peruvian Ceviche Nachos

Ingredients:

For the Ceviche:

- 1 lb fresh white fish fillets (such as sea bass, tilapia, or sole), diced into small pieces
- Juice of 4-5 limes
- 1 red onion, finely chopped
- 1-2 hot peppers (aji amarillo or jalapeño), seeded and finely chopped
- 2-3 cloves garlic, minced
- 1/4 cup chopped cilantro
- 1-2 tomatoes, seeded and diced
- Salt, to taste
- Pepper, to taste

For the Nachos:

- Tortilla chips
- Shredded cheese (such as Monterey Jack or cheddar)
- Sliced jalapeños
- Sliced black olives
- Diced avocado
- Sour cream
- Salsa
- Lime wedges, for serving
- Additional chopped cilantro, for garnish

Instructions:

Prepare the Ceviche:
- In a large mixing bowl, combine the diced fish with the lime juice. Let it marinate for about 10-15 minutes until the fish turns opaque.
- Add the finely chopped red onion, hot peppers, minced garlic, chopped cilantro, and diced tomatoes to the fish mixture.

- Season with salt and pepper to taste. Stir well to combine all the ingredients. Set aside.

Assemble the Nachos:
- Preheat your oven to 375°F (190°C).
- Arrange the tortilla chips in a single layer on a large baking sheet.
- Sprinkle shredded cheese evenly over the tortilla chips.
- Spoon the prepared ceviche mixture over the cheese-topped tortilla chips.
- Top with sliced jalapeños and black olives.

Bake the Nachos:
- Place the baking sheet in the preheated oven and bake for about 10-15 minutes, or until the cheese is melted and bubbly.

Serve the Nachos:
- Remove the nachos from the oven and let them cool slightly.
- Garnish with diced avocado and dollops of sour cream.
- Drizzle salsa over the nachos or serve it on the side for dipping.
- Squeeze fresh lime juice over the nachos for an extra burst of flavor.
- Sprinkle additional chopped cilantro over the top for garnish.

Enjoy these delicious Peruvian Ceviche Nachos as a flavorful appetizer or snack, perfect for sharing with friends and family!

Peruvian Ceviche Crostinis

Ingredients:

For the Ceviche:

- 1 lb fresh white fish fillets (such as sea bass, tilapia, or sole), diced into small pieces
- Juice of 4-5 limes
- 1 red onion, finely chopped
- 1-2 hot peppers (aji amarillo or jalapeño), seeded and finely chopped
- 2-3 cloves garlic, minced
- 1/4 cup chopped cilantro
- 1-2 tomatoes, seeded and diced
- Salt, to taste
- Pepper, to taste

For the Crostinis:

- Baguette, sliced into 1/2 inch thick rounds
- Olive oil, for brushing
- Salt, to taste
- Pepper, to taste

For Assembly:

- Avocado slices
- Thinly sliced radishes
- Fresh cilantro leaves
- Lime wedges, for serving
- Optional: hot sauce or chili flakes for added heat

Instructions:

Prepare the Ceviche:
- In a large mixing bowl, combine the diced fish with the lime juice. Let it marinate for about 10-15 minutes until the fish turns opaque.

- Add the finely chopped red onion, hot peppers, minced garlic, chopped cilantro, and diced tomatoes to the fish mixture.
- Season with salt and pepper to taste. Stir well to combine all the ingredients. Set aside.

Prepare the Crostinis:
- Preheat your oven to 375°F (190°C).
- Arrange the baguette slices in a single layer on a baking sheet.
- Lightly brush each slice with olive oil and sprinkle with salt and pepper.
- Bake in the preheated oven for about 8-10 minutes, or until the crostinis are golden brown and crispy. Remove from the oven and let them cool slightly.

Assemble the Crostinis:
- Top each crostini with a spoonful of the prepared ceviche mixture.
- Garnish with avocado slices, thinly sliced radishes, and fresh cilantro leaves.
- Squeeze a lime wedge over each crostini for an extra burst of citrus flavor.
- Optionally, drizzle with hot sauce or sprinkle with chili flakes for added heat.

Serve the Peruvian Ceviche Crostinis immediately as a flavorful and elegant appetizer, perfect for any occasion.

Enjoy these delicious Peruvian Ceviche Crostinis with friends and family, savoring the bright and refreshing flavors with each bite!

Peruvian Ceviche Bruschetta

Ingredients:

For the Ceviche:

- 1 lb fresh white fish fillets (such as sea bass, tilapia, or sole), diced into small pieces
- Juice of 4-5 limes
- 1 red onion, finely chopped
- 1-2 hot peppers (aji amarillo or jalapeño), seeded and finely chopped
- 2-3 cloves garlic, minced
- 1/4 cup chopped cilantro
- 1-2 tomatoes, seeded and diced
- Salt, to taste
- Pepper, to taste

For the Bruschetta:

- Baguette, sliced into 1/2 inch thick rounds
- Olive oil, for brushing
- Salt, to taste
- Pepper, to taste

For Assembly:

- Avocado slices
- Thinly sliced radishes
- Fresh cilantro leaves
- Lime wedges, for serving
- Optional: hot sauce or chili flakes for added heat

Instructions:

Prepare the Ceviche:
- In a large mixing bowl, combine the diced fish with the lime juice. Let it marinate for about 10-15 minutes until the fish turns opaque.
- Add the finely chopped red onion, hot peppers, minced garlic, chopped cilantro, and diced tomatoes to the fish mixture.

- Season with salt and pepper to taste. Stir well to combine all the ingredients. Set aside.

Prepare the Bruschetta:
- Preheat your oven to 375°F (190°C).
- Arrange the baguette slices in a single layer on a baking sheet.
- Lightly brush each slice with olive oil and sprinkle with salt and pepper.
- Bake in the preheated oven for about 8-10 minutes, or until the bruschetta slices are golden brown and crispy. Remove from the oven and let them cool slightly.

Assemble the Peruvian Ceviche Bruschetta:
- Top each bruschetta slice with a spoonful of the prepared ceviche mixture.
- Garnish with avocado slices, thinly sliced radishes, and fresh cilantro leaves.
- Squeeze a lime wedge over each bruschetta for an extra burst of citrus flavor.
- Optionally, drizzle with hot sauce or sprinkle with chili flakes for added heat.

Serve the Peruvian Ceviche Bruschetta immediately as a flavorful and elegant appetizer, perfect for any occasion.

Enjoy these delicious Peruvian Ceviche Bruschetta with friends and family, savoring the bright and refreshing flavors with each bite!

Peruvian Ceviche Stuffed Potato Skins

Ingredients:

For the Ceviche:

- 1 lb fresh white fish fillets (such as sea bass, tilapia, or sole), diced into small pieces
- Juice of 4-5 limes
- 1 red onion, finely chopped
- 1-2 hot peppers (aji amarillo or jalapeño), seeded and finely chopped
- 2-3 cloves garlic, minced
- 1/4 cup chopped cilantro
- 1-2 tomatoes, seeded and diced
- Salt, to taste
- Pepper, to taste

For the Potato Skins:

- 4 large russet potatoes
- Olive oil, for brushing
- Salt, to taste
- Pepper, to taste
- Shredded cheese (such as Monterey Jack or cheddar), for topping

For Assembly:

- Avocado slices
- Thinly sliced radishes
- Fresh cilantro leaves
- Lime wedges, for serving
- Optional: hot sauce or chili flakes for added heat

Instructions:

Prepare the Ceviche:

- In a large mixing bowl, combine the diced fish with the lime juice. Let it marinate for about 10-15 minutes until the fish turns opaque.
- Add the finely chopped red onion, hot peppers, minced garlic, chopped cilantro, and diced tomatoes to the fish mixture.
- Season with salt and pepper to taste. Stir well to combine all the ingredients. Set aside.

Prepare the Potato Skins:
- Preheat your oven to 400°F (200°C).
- Scrub the potatoes clean and pat them dry with a paper towel.
- Prick each potato several times with a fork.
- Rub the potatoes with olive oil and sprinkle with salt and pepper.
- Place the potatoes on a baking sheet and bake in the preheated oven for about 45-60 minutes, or until tender when pierced with a fork.
- Remove the potatoes from the oven and let them cool slightly.

Cut the potatoes in half lengthwise and scoop out the flesh, leaving about 1/4 inch of potato attached to the skin. Reserve the potato flesh for another use.

Assemble the Peruvian Ceviche Stuffed Potato Skins:
- Fill each potato skin with a generous spoonful of the prepared ceviche mixture.
- Top with shredded cheese.
- Place the stuffed potato skins back on the baking sheet and return them to the oven.
- Bake for an additional 5-10 minutes, or until the cheese is melted and bubbly.

Serve the Peruvian Ceviche Stuffed Potato Skins immediately, garnished with avocado slices, thinly sliced radishes, and fresh cilantro leaves.

Serve with lime wedges on the side for squeezing and optional hot sauce or chili flakes for added heat.

Enjoy these flavorful and satisfying Peruvian Ceviche Stuffed Potato Skins as a delicious appetizer or snack!

Peruvian Ceviche Lettuce Cups

Ingredients:

For the Ceviche:

- 1 lb fresh white fish fillets (such as sea bass, tilapia, or sole), diced into small pieces
- Juice of 4-5 limes
- 1 red onion, finely chopped
- 1-2 hot peppers (aji amarillo or jalapeño), seeded and finely chopped
- 2-3 cloves garlic, minced
- 1/4 cup chopped cilantro
- 1-2 tomatoes, seeded and diced
- Salt, to taste
- Pepper, to taste

For Assembly:

- Large lettuce leaves (such as romaine or butter lettuce)
- Avocado slices
- Thinly sliced radishes
- Fresh cilantro leaves
- Lime wedges, for serving
- Optional: hot sauce or chili flakes for added heat

Instructions:

    Prepare the Ceviche:
- In a large mixing bowl, combine the diced fish with the lime juice. Let it marinate for about 10-15 minutes until the fish turns opaque.
- Add the finely chopped red onion, hot peppers, minced garlic, chopped cilantro, and diced tomatoes to the fish mixture.
- Season with salt and pepper to taste. Stir well to combine all the ingredients. Set aside.

    Assemble the Lettuce Cups:
- Take a large lettuce leaf and place a spoonful of the prepared ceviche mixture in the center.

- Top the ceviche with avocado slices, thinly sliced radishes, and fresh cilantro leaves.
- Squeeze a lime wedge over the top for an extra burst of citrus flavor.
- Optionally, drizzle with hot sauce or sprinkle with chili flakes for added heat.

Repeat the process with the remaining lettuce leaves and ceviche mixture until all the ingredients are used.

Serve the Peruvian Ceviche Lettuce Cups immediately as a light and flavorful appetizer, perfect for any occasion.

Enjoy these delicious and refreshing Peruvian Ceviche Lettuce Cups with friends and family, savoring the bright and vibrant flavors with each bite!

Peruvian Ceviche Tostones

Ingredients:

For the Ceviche:

- 1 lb fresh white fish fillets (such as sea bass, tilapia, or sole), diced into small pieces
- Juice of 4-5 limes
- 1 red onion, finely chopped
- 1-2 hot peppers (aji amarillo or jalapeño), seeded and finely chopped
- 2-3 cloves garlic, minced
- 1/4 cup chopped cilantro
- 1-2 tomatoes, seeded and diced
- Salt, to taste
- Pepper, to taste

For the Tostones:

- 2 green plantains, peeled and sliced into 1-inch thick rounds
- Vegetable oil, for frying
- Salt, to taste

For Assembly:

- Avocado slices
- Thinly sliced radishes
- Fresh cilantro leaves
- Lime wedges, for serving
- Optional: hot sauce or chili flakes for added heat

Instructions:

Prepare the Ceviche:
- In a large mixing bowl, combine the diced fish with the lime juice. Let it marinate for about 10-15 minutes until the fish turns opaque.

- Add the finely chopped red onion, hot peppers, minced garlic, chopped cilantro, and diced tomatoes to the fish mixture.
- Season with salt and pepper to taste. Stir well to combine all the ingredients. Set aside.

Prepare the Tostones:
- In a large skillet, heat vegetable oil over medium-high heat.
- Fry the plantain slices in batches until golden brown and crispy, about 2-3 minutes per side.
- Remove the fried plantains from the oil and transfer them to a paper towel-lined plate to drain excess oil.
- Using a tostone press or the bottom of a flat, heavy object, flatten each fried plantain slice to about 1/4 inch thickness.
- Return the flattened plantains to the hot oil and fry for an additional 1-2 minutes on each side, until golden brown and crisp.
- Remove the tostones from the oil and place them on a paper towel-lined plate. Sprinkle with salt while they are still hot.

Assemble the Peruvian Ceviche Tostones:
- Top each tostone with a spoonful of the prepared ceviche mixture.
- Garnish with avocado slices, thinly sliced radishes, and fresh cilantro leaves.
- Squeeze a lime wedge over the top for an extra burst of citrus flavor.
- Optionally, drizzle with hot sauce or sprinkle with chili flakes for added heat.

Serve the Peruvian Ceviche Tostones immediately as a flavorful and satisfying appetizer or snack.

Enjoy these delicious Peruvian Ceviche Tostones with friends and family, savoring the crispy texture of the plantains paired with the zesty ceviche topping!

Peruvian Ceviche Skewers

Ingredients:

For the Ceviche:

- 1 lb fresh white fish fillets (such as sea bass, tilapia, or sole), diced into small pieces
- Juice of 4-5 limes
- 1 red onion, finely chopped
- 1-2 hot peppers (aji amarillo or jalapeño), seeded and finely chopped
- 2-3 cloves garlic, minced
- 1/4 cup chopped cilantro
- 1-2 tomatoes, seeded and diced
- Salt, to taste
- Pepper, to taste

For the Skewers:

- Bamboo skewers, soaked in water for at least 30 minutes to prevent burning
- Cherry tomatoes
- Avocado chunks
- Thinly sliced radishes
- Fresh cilantro leaves
- Lime wedges, for serving
- Optional: hot sauce or chili flakes for added heat

Instructions:

Prepare the Ceviche:
- In a large mixing bowl, combine the diced fish with the lime juice. Let it marinate for about 10-15 minutes until the fish turns opaque.
- Add the finely chopped red onion, hot peppers, minced garlic, chopped cilantro, and diced tomatoes to the fish mixture.
- Season with salt and pepper to taste. Stir well to combine all the ingredients. Set aside.

Assemble the Skewers:

- Thread the marinated fish onto the soaked bamboo skewers, alternating with cherry tomatoes, avocado chunks, and thinly sliced radishes.
- Continue threading until each skewer is filled with a colorful assortment of ceviche ingredients.
- Place the assembled skewers on a serving platter.

Serve the Peruvian Ceviche Skewers:
- Garnish the skewers with fresh cilantro leaves and lime wedges.
- Optionally, drizzle with hot sauce or sprinkle with chili flakes for added heat.
- Serve the skewers immediately as a vibrant and flavorful appetizer, perfect for any occasion.

Enjoy these delicious Peruvian Ceviche Skewers with friends and family, savoring the combination of zesty ceviche with fresh and colorful ingredients!

Peruvian Ceviche Sandwiches

Ingredients:

For the Ceviche:

- 1 lb fresh white fish fillets (such as sea bass, tilapia, or sole), diced into small pieces
- Juice of 4-5 limes
- 1 red onion, finely chopped
- 1-2 hot peppers (aji amarillo or jalapeño), seeded and finely chopped
- 2-3 cloves garlic, minced
- 1/4 cup chopped cilantro
- 1-2 tomatoes, seeded and diced
- Salt, to taste
- Pepper, to taste

For the Sandwiches:

- French baguette or your favorite sandwich bread
- Mayonnaise
- Avocado slices
- Thinly sliced radishes
- Lettuce leaves
- Fresh cilantro leaves
- Lime wedges, for serving
- Optional: hot sauce or chili flakes for added heat

Instructions:

Prepare the Ceviche:
- In a large mixing bowl, combine the diced fish with the lime juice. Let it marinate for about 10-15 minutes until the fish turns opaque.
- Add the finely chopped red onion, hot peppers, minced garlic, chopped cilantro, and diced tomatoes to the fish mixture.
- Season with salt and pepper to taste. Stir well to combine all the ingredients. Set aside.

Assemble the Sandwiches:
- Slice the baguette or sandwich bread lengthwise and spread mayonnaise on both sides.
- Layer the bottom half of the bread with avocado slices, thinly sliced radishes, and lettuce leaves.
- Spoon the prepared ceviche mixture on top of the vegetables.
- Garnish with fresh cilantro leaves and squeeze a lime wedge over the ceviche.

Close the sandwiches with the top half of the bread.

Serve the Peruvian Ceviche Sandwiches immediately as a delicious and satisfying meal, perfect for lunch or dinner.

Enjoy these flavorful Peruvian Ceviche Sandwiches with friends and family, savoring the bright and zesty flavors with every bite!

Peruvian Ceviche Wraps

Ingredients:

For the Ceviche:

- 1 lb fresh white fish fillets (such as sea bass, tilapia, or sole), diced into small pieces
- Juice of 4-5 limes
- 1 red onion, finely chopped
- 1-2 hot peppers (aji amarillo or jalapeño), seeded and finely chopped
- 2-3 cloves garlic, minced
- 1/4 cup chopped cilantro
- 1-2 tomatoes, seeded and diced
- Salt, to taste
- Pepper, to taste

For the Wraps:

- Large flour tortillas or your favorite wraps
- Avocado slices
- Shredded lettuce
- Thinly sliced radishes
- Fresh cilantro leaves
- Lime wedges, for serving
- Optional: hot sauce or chili flakes for added heat

Instructions:

Prepare the Ceviche:
- In a large mixing bowl, combine the diced fish with the lime juice. Let it marinate for about 10-15 minutes until the fish turns opaque.
- Add the finely chopped red onion, hot peppers, minced garlic, chopped cilantro, and diced tomatoes to the fish mixture.
- Season with salt and pepper to taste. Stir well to combine all the ingredients. Set aside.

Assemble the Wraps:

- Lay a large flour tortilla or wrap on a clean surface.
- Place a layer of shredded lettuce in the center of the tortilla.
- Spoon the prepared ceviche mixture on top of the lettuce.
- Add avocado slices, thinly sliced radishes, and fresh cilantro leaves on top of the ceviche.

Squeeze a lime wedge over the filling for an extra burst of citrus flavor.

Optional: Drizzle with hot sauce or sprinkle with chili flakes for added heat.

Fold the sides of the tortilla inward, then roll it up tightly to form a wrap.

Slice the wrap in half diagonally, if desired, and serve immediately.

Serve the Peruvian Ceviche Wraps with extra lime wedges on the side for squeezing.

Enjoy these delicious and refreshing wraps as a satisfying meal or snack, perfect for any occasion!

Peruvian Ceviche Canapés

Ingredients:

For the Ceviche:

- 1 lb fresh white fish fillets (such as sea bass, tilapia, or sole), diced into small pieces
- Juice of 4-5 limes
- 1 red onion, finely chopped
- 1-2 hot peppers (aji amarillo or jalapeño), seeded and finely chopped
- 2-3 cloves garlic, minced
- 1/4 cup chopped cilantro
- 1-2 tomatoes, seeded and diced
- Salt, to taste
- Pepper, to taste

For the Canapés:

- Baguette or sliced bread, cut into thin rounds or squares
- Olive oil, for brushing
- Avocado slices
- Thinly sliced radishes
- Fresh cilantro leaves
- Lime wedges, for serving
- Optional: hot sauce or chili flakes for added heat

Instructions:

Prepare the Ceviche:
- In a large mixing bowl, combine the diced fish with the lime juice. Let it marinate for about 10-15 minutes until the fish turns opaque.
- Add the finely chopped red onion, hot peppers, minced garlic, chopped cilantro, and diced tomatoes to the fish mixture.
- Season with salt and pepper to taste. Stir well to combine all the ingredients. Set aside.

Prepare the Bread:
- Preheat your oven to 375°F (190°C).
- Arrange the baguette rounds or bread slices on a baking sheet.

- Lightly brush each piece with olive oil.
- Bake in the preheated oven for about 8-10 minutes, or until the bread is toasted and crispy. Remove from the oven and let them cool slightly.

Assemble the Canapés:
- Top each toasted bread round or slice with a spoonful of the prepared ceviche mixture.
- Garnish with avocado slices, thinly sliced radishes, and fresh cilantro leaves.
- Squeeze a lime wedge over each canapé for an extra burst of citrus flavor.
- Optionally, drizzle with hot sauce or sprinkle with chili flakes for added heat.

Serve the Peruvian Ceviche Canapés immediately as an elegant and flavorful appetizer, perfect for any gathering or celebration.

Enjoy these delicious and visually appealing canapés with friends and family, savoring the vibrant flavors of Peruvian ceviche in every bite!

Peruvian Ceviche Dip

Ingredients:

For the Ceviche:

- 1 lb fresh white fish fillets (such as sea bass, tilapia, or sole), diced into small pieces
- Juice of 4-5 limes
- 1 red onion, finely chopped
- 1-2 hot peppers (aji amarillo or jalapeño), seeded and finely chopped
- 2-3 cloves garlic, minced
- 1/4 cup chopped cilantro
- 1-2 tomatoes, seeded and diced
- Salt, to taste
- Pepper, to taste

For the Dip:

- 8 oz cream cheese, softened
- 1/2 cup sour cream
- 1/4 cup mayonnaise
- 1 tablespoon lime juice
- 1/4 teaspoon ground cumin
- Salt, to taste
- Pepper, to taste
- Optional toppings: diced avocado, sliced radishes, chopped cilantro, lime wedges

Instructions:

Prepare the Ceviche:
- In a large mixing bowl, combine the diced fish with the lime juice. Let it marinate for about 10-15 minutes until the fish turns opaque.
- Add the finely chopped red onion, hot peppers, minced garlic, chopped cilantro, and diced tomatoes to the fish mixture.
- Season with salt and pepper to taste. Stir well to combine all the ingredients. Set aside.

Prepare the Dip:
- In a separate mixing bowl, beat the softened cream cheese until smooth and creamy.
- Add the sour cream, mayonnaise, lime juice, and ground cumin to the cream cheese. Mix until well combined.
- Season the dip with salt and pepper to taste. Adjust seasoning as needed.

Assemble the Dip:
- Spread the prepared cream cheese mixture evenly onto the bottom of a serving dish or shallow bowl.
- Spoon the prepared ceviche mixture on top of the cream cheese layer, spreading it out evenly.

Optional: Top the ceviche dip with diced avocado, sliced radishes, chopped cilantro, and lime wedges for garnish.

Serve the Peruvian Ceviche Dip immediately with tortilla chips, crackers, or vegetable sticks for dipping.

Enjoy this flavorful and creamy dip at your next party or gathering, and watch it disappear in no time!

Peruvian Ceviche Cucumber Bites

Ingredients:

For the Ceviche:

- 1 lb fresh white fish fillets (such as sea bass, tilapia, or sole), diced into small pieces
- Juice of 4-5 limes
- 1 red onion, finely chopped
- 1-2 hot peppers (aji amarillo or jalapeño), seeded and finely chopped
- 2-3 cloves garlic, minced
- 1/4 cup chopped cilantro
- 1-2 tomatoes, seeded and diced
- Salt, to taste
- Pepper, to taste

For the Cucumber Bites:

- English cucumbers, sliced into rounds
- Avocado slices
- Thinly sliced radishes
- Fresh cilantro leaves
- Lime wedges, for serving
- Optional: hot sauce or chili flakes for added heat

Instructions:

Prepare the Ceviche:
- In a large mixing bowl, combine the diced fish with the lime juice. Let it marinate for about 10-15 minutes until the fish turns opaque.
- Add the finely chopped red onion, hot peppers, minced garlic, chopped cilantro, and diced tomatoes to the fish mixture.
- Season with salt and pepper to taste. Stir well to combine all the ingredients. Set aside.

Assemble the Cucumber Bites:
- Slice the English cucumbers into rounds, about 1/2 inch thick.

- Arrange the cucumber rounds on a serving platter.
- Top each cucumber round with a spoonful of the prepared ceviche mixture.
- Garnish with avocado slices, thinly sliced radishes, and fresh cilantro leaves.
- Squeeze a lime wedge over each cucumber bite for an extra burst of citrus flavor.
- Optionally, drizzle with hot sauce or sprinkle with chili flakes for added heat.

Serve the Peruvian Ceviche Cucumber Bites immediately as a light and refreshing appetizer, perfect for any occasion.

Enjoy these delicious and colorful bites with friends and family, savoring the bright and zesty flavors of Peruvian ceviche in every bite!

Peruvian Ceviche Sopes

Ingredients:

For the Ceviche:

- 1 lb fresh white fish fillets (such as sea bass, tilapia, or sole), diced into small pieces
- Juice of 4-5 limes
- 1 red onion, finely chopped
- 1-2 hot peppers (aji amarillo or jalapeño), seeded and finely chopped
- 2-3 cloves garlic, minced
- 1/4 cup chopped cilantro
- 1-2 tomatoes, seeded and diced
- Salt, to taste
- Pepper, to taste

For the Sopes:

- 2 cups masa harina (corn flour)
- 1 1/4 cups warm water
- 1/2 teaspoon salt
- Vegetable oil, for frying

For Assembly:

- Avocado slices
- Thinly sliced radishes
- Fresh cilantro leaves
- Lime wedges, for serving
- Optional: hot sauce or chili flakes for added heat

Instructions:

Prepare the Ceviche:
- In a large mixing bowl, combine the diced fish with the lime juice. Let it marinate for about 10-15 minutes until the fish turns opaque.

- Add the finely chopped red onion, hot peppers, minced garlic, chopped cilantro, and diced tomatoes to the fish mixture.
- Season with salt and pepper to taste. Stir well to combine all the ingredients. Set aside.

Prepare the Sopes:
- In a large mixing bowl, combine the masa harina and salt. Gradually add the warm water, mixing until a soft dough forms.
- Divide the dough into golf ball-sized portions and flatten them into thick discs, about 1/4 inch thick.
- Heat vegetable oil in a skillet over medium heat. Fry the sopes in the hot oil until golden brown and cooked through, about 2-3 minutes per side. Drain on paper towels.

Assemble the Peruvian Ceviche Sopes:
- Top each cooked sope with a spoonful of the prepared ceviche mixture.
- Garnish with avocado slices, thinly sliced radishes, and fresh cilantro leaves.
- Squeeze a lime wedge over each sope for an extra burst of citrus flavor.
- Optionally, drizzle with hot sauce or sprinkle with chili flakes for added heat.

Serve the Peruvian Ceviche Sopes immediately as a flavorful and satisfying appetizer or snack.

Enjoy these delicious Peruvian Ceviche Sopes with friends and family, savoring the unique combination of flavors and textures!

Peruvian Ceviche Wontons

Ingredients:

For the Ceviche:

- 1 lb fresh white fish fillets (such as sea bass, tilapia, or sole), diced into small pieces
- Juice of 4-5 limes
- 1 red onion, finely chopped
- 1-2 hot peppers (aji amarillo or jalapeño), seeded and finely chopped
- 2-3 cloves garlic, minced
- 1/4 cup chopped cilantro
- 1-2 tomatoes, seeded and diced
- Salt, to taste
- Pepper, to taste

For the Wontons:

- Wonton wrappers
- Water, for sealing wontons
- Vegetable oil, for frying or baking

For Assembly:

- Avocado slices
- Thinly sliced radishes
- Fresh cilantro leaves
- Lime wedges, for serving
- Optional: hot sauce or chili flakes for added heat

Instructions:

Prepare the Ceviche:
- In a large mixing bowl, combine the diced fish with the lime juice. Let it marinate for about 10-15 minutes until the fish turns opaque.

- Add the finely chopped red onion, hot peppers, minced garlic, chopped cilantro, and diced tomatoes to the fish mixture.
- Season with salt and pepper to taste. Stir well to combine all the ingredients. Set aside.

Assemble the Wontons:
- Place a small spoonful of the ceviche mixture in the center of each wonton wrapper.
- Dip your finger in water and moisten the edges of the wonton wrapper.
- Fold the wonton wrapper diagonally to form a triangle, pressing the edges firmly to seal.
- Optionally, you can fold the two opposite corners together to create a small pouch shape.

Cooking Options:
- Deep-fry: Heat vegetable oil in a deep fryer or skillet to 350°F (175°C). Fry the wontons in batches until golden brown and crispy, about 2-3 minutes per batch. Drain on paper towels.
- Bake: Preheat your oven to 375°F (190°C). Place the assembled wontons on a baking sheet lined with parchment paper. Lightly brush the tops with oil. Bake for 12-15 minutes, or until golden brown and crispy.

Assemble the Peruvian Ceviche Wontons:
- Top the cooked wontons with avocado slices, thinly sliced radishes, and fresh cilantro leaves.
- Serve with lime wedges on the side for squeezing and optional hot sauce or chili flakes for added heat.

Enjoy these flavorful Peruvian Ceviche Wontons as a delicious appetizer or snack, combining the crispy texture of wontons with the zesty flavors of ceviche!

Peruvian Ceviche Bruschetta

Ingredients:

For the Ceviche:

- 1 lb fresh white fish fillets (such as sea bass, tilapia, or sole), diced into small pieces
- Juice of 4-5 limes
- 1 red onion, finely chopped
- 1-2 hot peppers (aji amarillo or jalapeño), seeded and finely chopped
- 2-3 cloves garlic, minced
- 1/4 cup chopped cilantro
- 1-2 tomatoes, seeded and diced
- Salt, to taste
- Pepper, to taste

For the Bruschetta:

- Baguette, sliced into rounds
- Olive oil, for brushing
- Garlic clove, peeled and halved
- Avocado slices
- Thinly sliced radishes
- Fresh cilantro leaves
- Lime wedges, for serving
- Optional: hot sauce or chili flakes for added heat

Instructions:

Prepare the Ceviche:
- In a large mixing bowl, combine the diced fish with the lime juice. Let it marinate for about 10-15 minutes until the fish turns opaque.
- Add the finely chopped red onion, hot peppers, minced garlic, chopped cilantro, and diced tomatoes to the fish mixture.
- Season with salt and pepper to taste. Stir well to combine all the ingredients. Set aside.

Prepare the Bruschetta:
- Preheat your oven to 375°F (190°C).
- Arrange the baguette slices on a baking sheet. Brush each slice with olive oil on both sides.
- Bake in the preheated oven for about 8-10 minutes, or until the bread is toasted and lightly golden brown.
- Remove the toasted baguette slices from the oven and rub each slice with the cut side of the garlic clove.

Assemble the Peruvian Ceviche Bruschetta:
- Spoon a generous amount of the prepared ceviche mixture onto each toasted baguette slice.
- Top with avocado slices, thinly sliced radishes, and fresh cilantro leaves.
- Squeeze a lime wedge over each bruschetta for an extra burst of citrus flavor.
- Optionally, drizzle with hot sauce or sprinkle with chili flakes for added heat.

Serve the Peruvian Ceviche Bruschetta immediately as a delicious and vibrant appetizer, perfect for any occasion.

Enjoy these flavorful and refreshing bruschetta with friends and family, savoring the unique fusion of Italian and Peruvian cuisines!

Peruvian Ceviche Pinchos

Ingredients:

For the Ceviche:

- 1 lb fresh white fish fillets (such as sea bass, tilapia, or sole), diced into small pieces
- Juice of 4-5 limes
- 1 red onion, finely chopped
- 1-2 hot peppers (aji amarillo or jalapeño), seeded and finely chopped
- 2-3 cloves garlic, minced
- 1/4 cup chopped cilantro
- 1-2 tomatoes, seeded and diced
- Salt, to taste
- Pepper, to taste

For the Pinchos:

- Bamboo skewers, soaked in water for at least 30 minutes
- Avocado slices
- Thinly sliced radishes
- Fresh cilantro leaves
- Lime wedges, for serving
- Optional: hot sauce or chili flakes for added heat

Instructions:

Prepare the Ceviche:
- In a large mixing bowl, combine the diced fish with the lime juice. Let it marinate for about 10-15 minutes until the fish turns opaque.
- Add the finely chopped red onion, hot peppers, minced garlic, chopped cilantro, and diced tomatoes to the fish mixture.
- Season with salt and pepper to taste. Stir well to combine all the ingredients. Set aside.

Assemble the Pinchos:
- Thread the marinated fish onto the soaked bamboo skewers, alternating with avocado slices and thinly sliced radishes.

- Continue threading until each skewer is filled with a colorful assortment of ceviche ingredients.
- Place the assembled pinchos on a serving platter.

Serve the Peruvian Ceviche Pinchos immediately as a vibrant and flavorful appetizer, perfect for any occasion.

Garnish with fresh cilantro leaves and lime wedges on the side for squeezing.

Optionally, drizzle with hot sauce or sprinkle with chili flakes for added heat.

Enjoy these delicious Peruvian Ceviche Pinchos with friends and family, savoring the unique fusion of flavors in every bite!

Peruvian Ceviche Pita Pockets

Ingredients:

For the Ceviche:

- 1 lb fresh white fish fillets (such as sea bass, tilapia, or sole), diced into small pieces
- Juice of 4-5 limes
- 1 red onion, finely chopped
- 1-2 hot peppers (aji amarillo or jalapeño), seeded and finely chopped
- 2-3 cloves garlic, minced
- 1/4 cup chopped cilantro
- 1-2 tomatoes, seeded and diced
- Salt, to taste
- Pepper, to taste

For the Pita Pockets:

- Whole wheat or regular pita bread rounds
- Lettuce leaves
- Sliced tomatoes
- Sliced cucumbers
- Sliced red onions
- Optional: sliced avocado, sliced radishes, chopped cilantro

Instructions:

Prepare the Ceviche:
- In a large mixing bowl, combine the diced fish with the lime juice. Let it marinate for about 10-15 minutes until the fish turns opaque.
- Add the finely chopped red onion, hot peppers, minced garlic, chopped cilantro, and diced tomatoes to the fish mixture.
- Season with salt and pepper to taste. Stir well to combine all the ingredients. Set aside.

Prepare the Pita Pockets:
- Warm the pita bread rounds in a toaster or oven until they are soft and pliable.
- Carefully open each pita pocket to create an opening for filling.

Assemble the Peruvian Ceviche Pita Pockets:
- Line the inside of each pita pocket with lettuce leaves.
- Spoon a generous amount of the prepared ceviche mixture into each pocket.
- Add sliced tomatoes, cucumbers, and red onions on top of the ceviche.
- Optionally, add sliced avocado, sliced radishes, and chopped cilantro for extra flavor and texture.

Serve the Peruvian Ceviche Pita Pockets immediately as a satisfying and flavorful meal or snack.

Enjoy these delicious and refreshing pita pockets with friends and family, savoring the vibrant flavors of Peruvian ceviche in every bite!

Peruvian Ceviche Sliders

Ingredients:

For the Ceviche:

- 1 lb fresh white fish fillets (such as sea bass, tilapia, or sole), diced into small pieces
- Juice of 4-5 limes
- 1 red onion, finely chopped
- 1-2 hot peppers (aji amarillo or jalapeño), seeded and finely chopped
- 2-3 cloves garlic, minced
- 1/4 cup chopped cilantro
- 1-2 tomatoes, seeded and diced
- Salt, to taste
- Pepper, to taste

For the Sliders:

- Slider buns or small dinner rolls
- Avocado slices
- Thinly sliced radishes
- Fresh cilantro leaves
- Lime wedges, for serving
- Optional: hot sauce or chili flakes for added heat

Instructions:

Prepare the Ceviche:
- In a large mixing bowl, combine the diced fish with the lime juice. Let it marinate for about 10-15 minutes until the fish turns opaque.
- Add the finely chopped red onion, hot peppers, minced garlic, chopped cilantro, and diced tomatoes to the fish mixture.
- Season with salt and pepper to taste. Stir well to combine all the ingredients. Set aside.

Assemble the Sliders:
- Slice the slider buns or dinner rolls in half horizontally.
- Place a spoonful of the prepared ceviche mixture on the bottom half of each bun.

- Top with avocado slices, thinly sliced radishes, and fresh cilantro leaves.
- Squeeze a lime wedge over each slider for an extra burst of citrus flavor.
- Optionally, drizzle with hot sauce or sprinkle with chili flakes for added heat.

Cover each slider with the top half of the bun to form a sandwich.

Serve the Peruvian Ceviche Sliders immediately as a delicious and unique appetizer or meal.

Enjoy these flavorful sliders with friends and family, savoring the vibrant flavors of Peruvian ceviche in every bite!

Peruvian Ceviche Flatbreads

Ingredients:

For the Ceviche:

- 1 lb fresh white fish fillets (such as sea bass, tilapia, or sole), diced into small pieces
- Juice of 4-5 limes
- 1 red onion, finely chopped
- 1-2 hot peppers (aji amarillo or jalapeño), seeded and finely chopped
- 2-3 cloves garlic, minced
- 1/4 cup chopped cilantro
- 1-2 tomatoes, seeded and diced
- Salt, to taste
- Pepper, to taste

For the Flatbreads:

- 2 large flatbreads or naan breads
- Olive oil, for brushing
- Garlic powder, for sprinkling
- Salt, to taste
- Pepper, to taste

For Assembly:

- Avocado slices
- Thinly sliced radishes
- Fresh cilantro leaves
- Lime wedges, for serving
- Optional: hot sauce or chili flakes for added heat

Instructions:

Prepare the Ceviche:
- In a large mixing bowl, combine the diced fish with the lime juice. Let it marinate for about 10-15 minutes until the fish turns opaque.
- Add the finely chopped red onion, hot peppers, minced garlic, chopped cilantro, and diced tomatoes to the fish mixture.

- Season with salt and pepper to taste. Stir well to combine all the ingredients. Set aside.

Prepare the Flatbreads:
- Preheat your oven to 400°F (200°C).
- Place the flatbreads or naan breads on a baking sheet.
- Brush the surface of each flatbread with olive oil.
- Sprinkle garlic powder, salt, and pepper over the oiled surface.

Bake the flatbreads in the preheated oven for 8-10 minutes, or until they are crispy and lightly golden brown.

Assemble the Peruvian Ceviche Flatbreads:
- Spoon a generous amount of the prepared ceviche mixture onto each baked flatbread.
- Top with avocado slices, thinly sliced radishes, and fresh cilantro leaves.
- Squeeze a lime wedge over each flatbread for an extra burst of citrus flavor.
- Optionally, drizzle with hot sauce or sprinkle with chili flakes for added heat.

Slice the flatbreads into wedges or squares and serve immediately.

Enjoy these delicious Peruvian Ceviche Flatbreads as a flavorful and satisfying meal or appetizer, perfect for any occasion!

Peruvian Ceviche Popsicles

Ingredients:

For the Ceviche Base:

- 1 lb fresh white fish fillets (such as sea bass, tilapia, or sole), diced into small pieces
- Juice of 4-5 limes
- 1 red onion, finely chopped
- 1-2 hot peppers (aji amarillo or jalapeño), seeded and finely chopped
- 2-3 cloves garlic, minced
- 1/4 cup chopped cilantro
- 1-2 tomatoes, seeded and diced
- Salt, to taste
- Pepper, to taste

For the Popsicles:

- Popsicle molds
- Popsicle sticks

Instructions:

Prepare the Ceviche Base:
- In a large mixing bowl, combine the diced fish with the lime juice. Let it marinate for about 10-15 minutes until the fish turns opaque.
- Add the finely chopped red onion, hot peppers, minced garlic, chopped cilantro, and diced tomatoes to the fish mixture.
- Season with salt and pepper to taste. Stir well to combine all the ingredients. Set aside.

Assemble the Popsicles:
- Spoon the prepared ceviche mixture into popsicle molds, filling each mold about 3/4 full.
- Insert popsicle sticks into the center of each mold.

Freeze the popsicles for at least 4-6 hours, or until completely frozen.

Once frozen, remove the popsicles from the molds by running warm water over the outside of the molds for a few seconds to loosen them.

Serve the Peruvian Ceviche Popsicles immediately as a refreshing and unexpected treat.

Enjoy these unique and flavorful popsicles with friends and family, savoring the vibrant flavors of ceviche in a frozen form!

Note: While this recipe offers a creative twist on traditional ceviche, be sure to use caution and consume the popsicles responsibly, especially if serving to guests who may not be familiar with this unconventional dessert.

Peruvian Ceviche Stuffed Mushrooms

Ingredients:

- 1 lb fresh white fish fillets (such as sea bass, tilapia, or sole), diced into small pieces
- Juice of 4-5 limes
- 1 red onion, finely chopped
- 1-2 hot peppers (aji amarillo or jalapeño), seeded and finely chopped
- 2-3 cloves garlic, minced
- 1/4 cup chopped cilantro
- 1-2 tomatoes, seeded and diced
- Salt, to taste
- Pepper, to taste
- 12-15 large mushrooms, stems removed and cleaned

Instructions:

Prepare the Ceviche Filling:
- In a large mixing bowl, combine the diced fish with the lime juice. Let it marinate for about 10-15 minutes until the fish turns opaque.
- Add the finely chopped red onion, hot peppers, minced garlic, chopped cilantro, and diced tomatoes to the fish mixture.
- Season with salt and pepper to taste. Stir well to combine all the ingredients. Set aside.

Preheat the oven to 375°F (190°C).

Stuff the Mushrooms:
- Arrange the cleaned mushroom caps on a baking sheet, cavity side up.
- Spoon a generous amount of the prepared ceviche mixture into each mushroom cap, pressing down gently to fill.

Bake the Stuffed Mushrooms:
- Place the baking sheet in the preheated oven and bake for 15-20 minutes, or until the mushrooms are tender and the ceviche filling is heated through.

Serve:
- Once baked, remove the stuffed mushrooms from the oven and let them cool slightly.
- Transfer the stuffed mushrooms to a serving platter and garnish with additional chopped cilantro, if desired.

Serve the Peruvian Ceviche Stuffed Mushrooms as a flavorful and elegant appetizer at your next gathering or special occasion.

Enjoy these delicious stuffed mushrooms with friends and family, savoring the unique combination of flavors in every bite!

Peruvian Ceviche Potato Salad

Ingredients:

For the Ceviche:

- 1 lb fresh white fish fillets (such as sea bass, tilapia, or sole), diced into small pieces
- Juice of 4-5 limes
- 1 red onion, finely chopped
- 1-2 hot peppers (aji amarillo or jalapeño), seeded and finely chopped
- 2-3 cloves garlic, minced
- 1/4 cup chopped cilantro
- 1-2 tomatoes, seeded and diced
- Salt, to taste
- Pepper, to taste

For the Potato Salad:

- 2 lbs potatoes (Yukon Gold or red potatoes), peeled and diced
- 1/4 cup mayonnaise
- 2 tablespoons sour cream
- 1 tablespoon Dijon mustard
- 1 tablespoon lime juice
- Salt, to taste
- Pepper, to taste
- Optional: chopped green onions, chopped cilantro, sliced radishes for garnish

Instructions:

Prepare the Ceviche:
- In a large mixing bowl, combine the diced fish with the lime juice. Let it marinate for about 10-15 minutes until the fish turns opaque.
- Add the finely chopped red onion, hot peppers, minced garlic, chopped cilantro, and diced tomatoes to the fish mixture.
- Season with salt and pepper to taste. Stir well to combine all the ingredients. Set aside.

Cook the Potatoes:
- Place the diced potatoes in a large pot of salted water.

- Bring the water to a boil and cook the potatoes until fork-tender, about 10-15 minutes.
- Drain the potatoes and let them cool slightly.

Prepare the Dressing:
- In a small bowl, whisk together the mayonnaise, sour cream, Dijon mustard, and lime juice until smooth.
- Season with salt and pepper to taste.

Assemble the Potato Salad:
- In a large mixing bowl, combine the cooked and slightly cooled potatoes with the ceviche mixture.
- Pour the prepared dressing over the potato and ceviche mixture, tossing gently to coat evenly.

Garnish and Serve:
- Garnish the Peruvian Ceviche Potato Salad with chopped green onions, chopped cilantro, and sliced radishes, if desired.
- Chill the potato salad in the refrigerator for at least 1 hour before serving to allow the flavors to meld together.

Serve the Peruvian Ceviche Potato Salad as a flavorful and refreshing side dish at your next barbecue, picnic, or gathering.

Enjoy this unique and delicious potato salad with friends and family, savoring the bright and zesty flavors of ceviche!

Peruvian Ceviche Deviled Eggs

Ingredients:

For the Ceviche:

- 1 lb fresh white fish fillets (such as sea bass, tilapia, or sole), diced into small pieces
- Juice of 4-5 limes
- 1 red onion, finely chopped
- 1-2 hot peppers (aji amarillo or jalapeño), seeded and finely chopped
- 2-3 cloves garlic, minced
- 1/4 cup chopped cilantro
- 1-2 tomatoes, seeded and diced
- Salt, to taste
- Pepper, to taste

For the Deviled Eggs:

- 6 hard-boiled eggs, peeled and halved lengthwise
- 2 tablespoons mayonnaise
- 1 teaspoon Dijon mustard
- 1 teaspoon lime juice
- Salt, to taste
- Pepper, to taste
- Optional: chopped cilantro, sliced radishes for garnish

Instructions:

Prepare the Ceviche:
- In a large mixing bowl, combine the diced fish with the lime juice. Let it marinate for about 10-15 minutes until the fish turns opaque.
- Add the finely chopped red onion, hot peppers, minced garlic, chopped cilantro, and diced tomatoes to the fish mixture.
- Season with salt and pepper to taste. Stir well to combine all the ingredients. Set aside.

Prepare the Deviled Egg Filling:

- Carefully remove the yolks from the hard-boiled eggs and place them in a separate bowl.
- Mash the egg yolks with a fork until smooth.
- Add mayonnaise, Dijon mustard, lime juice, salt, and pepper to the mashed yolks. Mix until well combined and creamy.

Assemble the Peruvian Ceviche Deviled Eggs:
- Spoon a small amount of the ceviche mixture into each egg white half, filling the cavity.
- Top each ceviche-filled egg half with a dollop of the deviled egg filling.

Garnish and Serve:
- Garnish the Peruvian Ceviche Deviled Eggs with chopped cilantro and sliced radishes, if desired.
- Serve the deviled eggs chilled as a flavorful and elegant appetizer at your next gathering or special occasion.

Enjoy these unique and delicious deviled eggs with friends and family, savoring the bright and zesty flavors of ceviche in every bite!

Peruvian Ceviche Gazpacho

Ingredients:

For the Ceviche:

- 1 lb fresh white fish fillets (such as sea bass, tilapia, or sole), diced into small pieces
- Juice of 4-5 limes
- 1 red onion, finely chopped
- 1-2 hot peppers (aji amarillo or jalapeño), seeded and finely chopped
- 2-3 cloves garlic, minced
- 1/4 cup chopped cilantro
- 1-2 tomatoes, seeded and diced
- Salt, to taste
- Pepper, to taste

For the Gazpacho Base:

- 4 large ripe tomatoes, roughly chopped
- 1 cucumber, peeled and roughly chopped
- 1 red bell pepper, seeded and roughly chopped
- 1/4 red onion, roughly chopped
- 2 cloves garlic, minced
- 1/4 cup fresh cilantro leaves
- 1/4 cup olive oil
- 2 tablespoons red wine vinegar
- Salt, to taste
- Pepper, to taste
- Optional: hot sauce or chili flakes for added heat

Instructions:

Prepare the Ceviche:
- In a large mixing bowl, combine the diced fish with the lime juice. Let it marinate for about 10-15 minutes until the fish turns opaque.

- Add the finely chopped red onion, hot peppers, minced garlic, chopped cilantro, and diced tomatoes to the fish mixture.
- Season with salt and pepper to taste. Stir well to combine all the ingredients. Set aside.

Prepare the Gazpacho Base:
- In a blender or food processor, combine the chopped tomatoes, cucumber, red bell pepper, red onion, garlic, and cilantro.
- Blend until smooth.
- With the blender running, slowly drizzle in the olive oil and red wine vinegar. Blend until well combined.
- Season the gazpacho base with salt and pepper to taste. Adjust seasoning as needed.
- Optionally, add hot sauce or chili flakes for added heat.

Assemble the Peruvian Ceviche Gazpacho:
- Divide the ceviche mixture among serving bowls.
- Pour the gazpacho base over the ceviche, covering it completely.
- Garnish with additional chopped cilantro, if desired.

Chill the Peruvian Ceviche Gazpacho in the refrigerator for at least 30 minutes before serving to allow the flavors to meld together and the soup to become cold. Serve the gazpacho cold as a refreshing and flavorful appetizer or light meal. Enjoy this unique and delicious Peruvian Ceviche Gazpacho, savoring the combination of refreshing gazpacho flavors with the zesty kick of ceviche!

Peruvian Ceviche Sushi Bowls

Ingredients:

For the Ceviche:

- 1 lb fresh white fish fillets (such as sea bass, tilapia, or sole), diced into small pieces
- Juice of 4-5 limes
- 1 red onion, finely chopped
- 1-2 hot peppers (aji amarillo or jalapeño), seeded and finely chopped
- 2-3 cloves garlic, minced
- 1/4 cup chopped cilantro
- 1-2 tomatoes, seeded and diced
- Salt, to taste
- Pepper, to taste

For the Sushi Bowls:

- Sushi rice, cooked according to package instructions
- Nori sheets, cut into thin strips
- Avocado slices
- Cucumber, thinly sliced
- Carrots, julienned
- Radishes, thinly sliced
- Pickled ginger, for serving
- Wasabi, for serving
- Soy sauce, for serving

Instructions:

Prepare the Ceviche:
- In a large mixing bowl, combine the diced fish with the lime juice. Let it marinate for about 10-15 minutes until the fish turns opaque.
- Add the finely chopped red onion, hot peppers, minced garlic, chopped cilantro, and diced tomatoes to the fish mixture.

- Season with salt and pepper to taste. Stir well to combine all the ingredients. Set aside.

Assemble the Sushi Bowls:
- Divide the cooked sushi rice among serving bowls.
- Arrange the ceviche mixture on top of the rice in each bowl.
- Add avocado slices, cucumber slices, julienned carrots, and thinly sliced radishes around the ceviche.

Garnish the bowls with nori strips.

Serve the Peruvian Ceviche Sushi Bowls with pickled ginger, wasabi, and soy sauce on the side.

Optionally, you can drizzle additional lime juice or a splash of soy sauce over the ceviche for extra flavor.

Enjoy these delicious and colorful sushi bowls, savoring the fusion of Japanese and Peruvian flavors in every bite!

These Peruvian Ceviche Sushi Bowls make for a satisfying and refreshing meal, perfect for lunch or dinner. Feel free to customize the toppings according to your preferences and enjoy the creative combination of ceviche and sushi in bowl form!

Peruvian Ceviche Sopes

Ingredients:

For the Ceviche:

- 1 lb fresh white fish fillets (such as sea bass, tilapia, or sole), diced into small pieces
- Juice of 4-5 limes
- 1 red onion, finely chopped
- 1-2 hot peppers (aji amarillo or jalapeño), seeded and finely chopped
- 2-3 cloves garlic, minced
- 1/4 cup chopped cilantro
- 1-2 tomatoes, seeded and diced
- Salt, to taste
- Pepper, to taste

For the Sopes:

- 1 cup masa harina (corn flour)
- 3/4 cup warm water
- Salt, to taste
- Vegetable oil, for frying
- Refried beans, for topping
- Avocado slices, for topping
- Radishes, thinly sliced, for topping
- Fresh cilantro leaves, for topping
- Lime wedges, for serving

Instructions:

Prepare the Ceviche:
- In a large mixing bowl, combine the diced fish with the lime juice. Let it marinate for about 10-15 minutes until the fish turns opaque.
- Add the finely chopped red onion, hot peppers, minced garlic, chopped cilantro, and diced tomatoes to the fish mixture.

- Season with salt and pepper to taste. Stir well to combine all the ingredients. Set aside.

Make the Sopes:
- In a mixing bowl, combine the masa harina and salt. Gradually add the warm water, mixing until a soft dough forms.
- Divide the dough into small balls, about the size of a golf ball.
- Flatten each ball into a disk, about 1/4 inch thick and 3 inches in diameter.
- Heat vegetable oil in a skillet over medium heat. Once hot, fry the sopes until golden brown and cooked through, about 2-3 minutes per side. Drain on paper towels.

Assemble the Peruvian Ceviche Sopes:
- Spread a layer of refried beans on each fried sope.
- Top with a spoonful of the prepared ceviche mixture.
- Garnish with avocado slices, thinly sliced radishes, and fresh cilantro leaves.

Serve the Peruvian Ceviche Sopes immediately, with lime wedges on the side for squeezing.

Enjoy these delicious and vibrant sopes as a flavorful appetizer or snack, savoring the fusion of Mexican and Peruvian flavors in every bite!

Peruvian Ceviche Bruschetta

Ingredients:

For the Ceviche:

- 1 lb fresh white fish fillets (such as sea bass, tilapia, or sole), diced into small pieces
- Juice of 4-5 limes
- 1 red onion, finely chopped
- 1-2 hot peppers (aji amarillo or jalapeño), seeded and finely chopped
- 2-3 cloves garlic, minced
- 1/4 cup chopped cilantro
- 1-2 tomatoes, seeded and diced
- Salt, to taste
- Pepper, to taste

For the Bruschetta:

- 1 baguette, thinly sliced
- Olive oil, for brushing
- 2 cloves garlic, peeled and halved
- Salt, to taste
- Pepper, to taste
- Optional: chopped fresh basil or parsley for garnish

Instructions:

Prepare the Ceviche:
- In a large mixing bowl, combine the diced fish with the lime juice. Let it marinate for about 10-15 minutes until the fish turns opaque.
- Add the finely chopped red onion, hot peppers, minced garlic, chopped cilantro, and diced tomatoes to the fish mixture.
- Season with salt and pepper to taste. Stir well to combine all the ingredients. Set aside.

Prepare the Bruschetta:
- Preheat the oven broiler.

- Place the baguette slices on a baking sheet and brush lightly with olive oil on both sides.
- Broil the bread slices for 1-2 minutes on each side, or until lightly golden brown.
- Remove the toasted baguette slices from the oven and rub each slice with a halved garlic clove. This will infuse the bread with garlic flavor.
- Season the toasted baguette slices with salt and pepper to taste.

Assemble the Peruvian Ceviche Bruschetta:
- Spoon a generous amount of the prepared ceviche mixture onto each toasted baguette slice.
- Garnish with chopped fresh basil or parsley, if desired.

Serve the Peruvian Ceviche Bruschetta immediately as a flavorful appetizer or snack.

Enjoy these delicious and vibrant bruschettas with friends and family, savoring the fusion of Italian and Peruvian flavors in every bite!

Peruvian Ceviche Stuffed Jalapeños

Ingredients:

For the Ceviche:

- 1 lb fresh white fish fillets (such as sea bass, tilapia, or sole), diced into small pieces
- Juice of 4-5 limes
- 1 red onion, finely chopped
- 1-2 hot peppers (aji amarillo or jalapeño), seeded and finely chopped
- 2-3 cloves garlic, minced
- 1/4 cup chopped cilantro
- 1-2 tomatoes, seeded and diced
- Salt, to taste
- Pepper, to taste

For the Stuffed Jalapeños:

- 12-15 fresh jalapeño peppers
- 4 oz cream cheese, softened
- 1/4 cup shredded cheddar or Monterey Jack cheese
- Optional: chopped cilantro or green onions for garnish

Instructions:

Prepare the Ceviche:
- In a large mixing bowl, combine the diced fish with the lime juice. Let it marinate for about 10-15 minutes until the fish turns opaque.
- Add the finely chopped red onion, hot peppers, minced garlic, chopped cilantro, and diced tomatoes to the fish mixture.
- Season with salt and pepper to taste. Stir well to combine all the ingredients. Set aside.

Prepare the Jalapeños:
- Preheat the oven to 375°F (190°C). Line a baking sheet with parchment paper.

- Slice the jalapeños in half lengthwise and remove the seeds and membranes using a spoon.

Make the Filling:
- In a small mixing bowl, combine the softened cream cheese and shredded cheese until well combined.

Assemble the Stuffed Jalapeños:
- Spoon a small amount of the ceviche mixture into each jalapeño half.
- Top the ceviche-filled jalapeños with the cream cheese mixture, filling each jalapeño half.

Bake the Stuffed Jalapeños:
- Place the stuffed jalapeños on the prepared baking sheet.
- Bake in the preheated oven for 15-20 minutes, or until the jalapeños are tender and the cheese is melted and bubbly.

Garnish and Serve:
- Optionally, garnish the stuffed jalapeños with chopped cilantro or green onions before serving.

Serve the Peruvian Ceviche Stuffed Jalapeños immediately as a spicy and flavorful appetizer or snack.

Enjoy these delicious stuffed jalapeños with friends and family, savoring the bold flavors of Peruvian ceviche in each bite!

www.ingramcontent.com/pod-product-compliance
Lightning Source LLC
LaVergne TN
LVHW081604060526
838201LV00054B/2071